AFRICAN-AMERICAN EDUCATORS

ELIZABETH MASSIE

TITLES IN THIS SERIES

AFRICAN-AMERICAN EDUCATORS

ELIZABETH MASSIE

MASON CREST
PHILADELPHIA

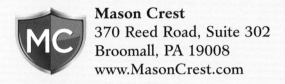

Mason Crest
370 Reed Road, Suite 302
Broomall, PA 19008
www.MasonCrest.com

Printed and bound in the United States of America.

CPSIA Compliance Information: Batch #MBC2012-3. For further information, contact Mason Crest at 1-866-MCP-Book.

First printing
1 3 5 7 9 8 6 4 2

Library of Congress Cataloging-in-Publication Data

Massie, Elizabeth.
  African American educators / Elizabeth Massie.
     pages cm. — (Major Black contributions from emancipation to civil rights)
  Includes bibliographical references and index.
  ISBN 978-1-4222-2373-4 (hc)
  ISBN 978-1-4222-2386-4 (pb)
  1. African American educators—Biography—Juvenile literature. I. Title.
  LA2311.M38 2012
  370.922—dc23
  [B]

                            2011051943

Publisher's note: All quotations in this book are taken from original sources, and contain the spelling and grammatical inconsistencies of the original texts.

Picture credits: courtesy Berea College: 34; courtesy East Carolina University: 17; Library of Congress: 3, 8, 14, 16, 18, 22, 23, 26, 29, 30, 32, 36, 39, 40, 43, 46, 48; courtesy Marva Collins Seminars: 51; © 2011 Photos.com, a division of Getty Images: 10; used under license from Shutterstock, Inc.: 7, 21, 59; Wikimedia Commons: 20.

TABLE OF CONTENTS

INTRODUCTION

Dr. Marc Lamont Hill

It is impossible to tell the story of America without telling the story of Black Americans. From the struggle to end slavery, all the way to the election of the first Black president, the Black experience has been a window into America's own movement toward becoming a "more perfect union." Through the tragedies and triumphs of Blacks in America, we gain a more full understanding of our collective history and a richer appreciation of our collective journey. This book series, MAJOR BLACK CONTRIBUTIONS FROM EMANCIPATION TO CIVIL RIGHTS, spotlights that journey by showing the many ways that Black Americans have been a central part of our nation's development.

In this series, we are reminded that Blacks were not merely objects of history, swept up in the winds of social and political inevitability. Rather, since the end of legal slavery, Black men and women have actively fought for their own rights and freedoms. It is through their courageous efforts (along with the efforts of allies of all races) that Blacks are able to enjoy ever increasing levels of inclusion in American democracy. Through this series, we learn the names and stories of some of the most important contributors to our democracy.

But this series goes far beyond the story of slavery to freedom. The books in this series also demonstrate the various contributions of Black Americans to the nation's social, cultural, technological, and intellectual growth. While these books provide new and deeper insights into the lives and stories of familiar figures like Martin Luther King, Michael Jordan, and Oprah Winfrey, they also introduce readers to the contributions of countless heroes who have often been pushed to the margins of history. In reading this series, we are able to see that Blacks have been key contributors across every field of human endeavor.

Although this is a series about Black Americans, it is important and necessary reading for everyone. While readers of color will find enormous purpose and pride in uncovering the history of their ancestors, these books should also create similar sentiments among readers of all races and ethnicities. By understanding the rich and deep history of Blacks, a group often ignored or marginalized in history, we are reminded that everyone has a story. Everyone has a contribution. Everyone matters.

The insights of these books are necessary for creating deeper, richer, and more inclusive classrooms. More importantly, they remind us of the power and possibility of individuals of all races, places, and traditions. Such insights not only allow us to understand the past, but to create a more beautiful future.

African-American children and adults stand outside a school for newly freed slaves, circa 1865. With the end of slavery after the Civil War, millions of African Americans who had not been allowed to attend school were able to learn how to read and write.

1

"DARK AND THORNY IS THE PATHWAY"

Imagine you have been invited to play a new board game with friends. You all sit down at the table. One friend rolls the dice. The game begins. As you watch, your friends move their pieces around the board. When it is your turn, you make a move—but your friends tell you you're doing it wrong. They skip over you and take their turns again, laughing and talking about how much fun they are having. Soon the game is over. One of your friends has won. You don't understand how, though. You didn't even know the rules of the game! You are upset. That was not fair. You weren't able to win. You weren't even able to play.

It has been said that knowledge is power. If you understood how to play the game, you would have had a better chance to succeed. Not knowing meant you couldn't even make a right move.

Learning new information and skills helps people succeed in life. Knowing how to read allows you to find facts and opinions in books, magazines, and on the internet. Reading also lets you enjoy stories and novels. Knowing how to write makes it possible for you to put your thought down to share with others. Learning about math, science, and history helps you understand the world around you.

AGAINST THE LAW TO LEARN

In the United States today, every young person can go to school and get an education. It doesn't matter whether you are rich, poor, or somewhere in the middle. It doesn't matter if you are a boy or girl. It doesn't matter what race you are. However, that hasn't always been true. At one time, there were people in our country who were not allowed to get an education. In fact, it was against the law for certain people to learn to read and write.

In 1607, Englishmen sailed across the Atlantic Ocean. They settled a town called Jamestown in Virginia. Twelve years later, the first Africans were brought to Jamestown on a Dutch ship. They did not want to come. They had been captured and forced onto the ship. They were sold to the settlers. Over the years that followed, more Africans were captured and brought to American colonies and sold.

At first, Africans were indentured servants. They worked for their masters for fourteen years. Then they were set free. By the middle of the century, however, all Africans in the colonies were considered slaves. They would have to serve their masters for their entire lives. Their children and other descendants would also be slaves.

Slaves pick cotton on a Southern plantation, 1850s. When the Civil War began in 1861, nearly 4 million African Americans were held in slavery. Their labor fueled the South's economy, which was based on cash crops like cotton, tobacco, and rice.

There were slaves in the Northern colonies and slaves in the Southern colonies. These enslaved people worked in fields, on shipping docks, and in shops, stables, barns, homes, and other places. In the earlier days, some slaves were taught to read and write by their masters. In this way, they were able to help with their masters' businesses.

In the South there was a lot of rich farmland. Some colonists established small farms. Others established large plantations. The warmer Southern climate was good for growing cash crops such as tobacco, cotton, and rice. Rich landowners needed a lot of people to work on their large plantations. Many of these workers were slaves. Slaves plowed the land and planted and harvested the crops. They cared for animals or worked at tasks such as bricklaying or carpentry. Still others, called house slaves, took care of the master's home by cleaning, cooking, or caring for the master's children.

> === Did You Know? ===
>
> Most slaves in America never got a formal education. Yet they learned and shared many things without reading and writing. They did this through songs, dances, and crafts.

There were very few schools for slaves in the South. These were usually run by religious leaders. However, most Southern slave owners did not want their slaves to be educated. Some feared slaves who could read and write would forge passes or freedom papers for themselves or others. They were afraid the slaves would write notes to other slaves and encourage them to run away or to revolt against their masters. Because of this, some laws were passed to keep slaves from getting an education.

Members of the Quaker faith believed slavery was wrong. They also believed that blacks should be given an equal chance to learn. Quakers in the North, most of whom were white, founded many schools for slaves and free blacks.

In 1776, the American colonies declared their freedom from England. They went to war. When the fighting was done, a new country was formed—the United States of America. This revolution was fought to gain

freedom. Yet it didn't bring freedom to everyone. Slaves were still slaves. Over time, the northern states outlawed slavery and set their slaves free. New Jersey was the last Northern state to abolish slavery in 1804. The leaders of the South, however, said they needed slaves to work on their farms and plantations. They did not set their slaves free.

In the South, authorities continued to resist slave education. Often, harsh punishments were used to prevent whites from teaching blacks. A law passed in Georgia in 1848 stated:

> Punishment for teaching slaves or free persons of color to read. —If any slave, Negro, or free person of color, or any white person, shall teach any other slave, Negro, or free person of color, to read or write either written or printed characters, the said free person of color or slave shall be punished by fine and whipping, or fine or whipping, at the discretion of the court.

LEARNING, ANYWAY

Lunsford Lane was born into slavery in North Carolina in 1803. He worked hard for his master during the day. At night, instead of resting, he earned his own money by selling peaches, wood, and tobacco. His master did not allow him to read. So Lane learned to read and write in secret. Later, he would state, "While in the South I succeeded by stealth in learning to read and write a little, and since I have been in the North I have learned more."

Sometimes, slaves who earned extra money were permitted to use it to purchase their freedom. By 1835 Lane's hard work had earned him enough money to buy his freedom. He moved to the North. He kept working until he could afford to pay for freedom for his wife and children. Lane wrote and published his life's story. It tells of his hardships and his successes.

Lunsford Lane is just one example of an enslaved person who, in spite of the dangers, found a way to get an education anyway.

Catherine "Katy" Ferguson was born into slavery in New York City in 1779. When she was eight, her mother was sold away from her. Katy knew she wanted to gain her freedom and get an education. She also wanted to help other slaves.

Katy asked her mistress to teach her to read. Her mistress refused. Katy kept on working. She hoped things would change. When she was sixteen, a kind lady paid $200 for Katy's freedom. Katy promised to pay her back. Eventually she did. Katy made a living for herself by baking cakes.

Education was still important to Katy. She opened her home to children on Sundays. There, they were taught how to read. Though she was not able to read or write herself, Katy brought in others to teach the children. She also let poor children move in with her. They were in great need of food, shelter, and clothes. Over time she cared for 48 children. Twenty of them were white.

Lily Ann Granderson, also known as Milla Granson, was born in Virginia in 1816. She was a slave. As a child, she moved to Kentucky. There, her master's children taught her to read and write. She was later sold to a slave owner in Natchez Mississippi. She had to work in the fields and was often whipped. She said, "O, how I longed to die! And sometimes I thought I would die from such cruel whippings upon my bared body."

After a while, Lily was moved from the field to work in the house. There, she set up a secret night school for slaves. They kept the doors and windows shut so no one could see them. Some of her students were able to write their own

> === Did You Know? ===
>
> In 1818, the Pennsylvania Augustine Society was formed by free blacks. It was a group that supported education for African Americans.

passes and escape to Canada, where slavery was outlawed in the 1830s. She continued to teach for many years, through the Civil War, and afterward.

FREEDOM ON THE HORIZON

While slave owners didn't want their slaves to be taught to read books, they wanted slaves to learn about the Bible. Southern slave owners liked Bible passages that said slaves should obey their masters. They thought knowing these passages would keep the slaves from rebelling. However, there was also a story in the Bible about Moses. Moses led his people to freedom out of slavery in Egypt. Slaves loved the story of Moses. It told of a distant, promised land where slaves could be free.

To hundreds of Southern slaves, Moses came in the form of a woman named Harriet Tubman. Tubman was a runaway slave herself who had escaped to the North. She sneaked back into the South 19 times. She led more than 300 Southern slaves to freedom. Tubman knew the dangers. The escaping slaves also knew the dangers. Yet they believed that being free was worth it. They wanted to make a living. They wanted to get an education.

Harriet had a special song she sang to let slaves know she would lead them to freedom. It offered hope to the runaways:

"Dark and thorny is the pathway
    Where the sinner makes his way
But beyond this vale of sorrow
    Lies the path to endless day."

By the mid-1800s, there was a lot of tension between the northern and southern states. The main disagreement was over slavery. In early 1861, southern states declared their independence from the United States of America. They had decided to start their own country, the Confederate States of America. Soon after, the Civil War began.

Harriet Tubman (1820?–1913) was nicknamed "Moses" for her furtive work helping African-American slaves escape to the North during the 1850s and 1860s.

2

TIME OF TRIAL
EDUCATION DURING
AND AFTER THE CIVIL WAR

The American Civil War lasted from 1861 to 1865. It was a terrible time. More than 600,000 Union and Confederate soldiers died. Some were killed in battle. Others died from disease. Cities were burned. Farms and crops were destroyed. Yet through that terrible time, people did their best to get on with their lives. In many parts of the South, slaves continued to work for their masters. In secret, small schools continued to give lessons to African-American slaves who were lucky enough to attend.

Charlotte Forten was a young African-American woman. She taught school in Massachusetts. She decided to help people in the South. In 1862 she left home. She traveled to St. Helena Island in South Carolina. There, she taught in a school for young children. It was a difficult job. Many of the children did not speak English. They spoke Gullah. The Gullah language is a mix of English and African languages. Still, Forten noted that the slaves of the area had "so great a desire for knowledge" that she was determined to help them. Later, in her book *Life on the Sea Islands*, she wrote:

> The first day of school was rather trying. Most of my children are very small, and consequently restless. But after some days of positive, though not severe, treatment, order was brought out of chaos. I never before saw children so eager to learn.

Charlotte Forten (1837–1914) was born to a family of free blacks in Philadelphia, and was educated at a private school in Massachusetts. After serving as a teacher and nurse in South Carolina, she worked in Washington, D.C., recruiting teachers. In 1878 she married a white abolitionist, Francis Grimké. Until her death, she worked for racial equality and

Charlotte Forten taught in South Carolina for two years. Then she became ill. She returned to the North. Forten was the first African American from the North to go to the South during the war to teach former slaves.

NEW DREAMS

On January 1, 1863, President Abraham Lincoln issued the Emancipation Proclamation. This paper freed some slaves. Yet it did not free them all. In December 1865, all slaves were officially freed when the Thirteenth Amendment to the U.S. Constitution was ratified.

African-American dreams of freedom had at last come true. Blacks no longer had to work for a master. They no longer would be sold or bought. Now, they could work for themselves. They were free to go where they wanted to go. They were free to get an education if they wanted one.

Freed slaves owned very little. Some had no more than the clothes they wore. Most did not know how to make a living, other than working in the fields. Many did not know how to read or write. They had never learned to handle money. It was a good time because they were free. Yet it was a hard time because they had many challenges ahead.

The Freedman's Bureau was set up in 1865. It was created by Congress to help former slaves become full citizens. The Bureau gave former slaves food and clothes. It helped them find family members that had been sold away. It helped them find homes, work, and get an education.

Bureau members were surprised to find there were already secret schools for slaves across the South. In fact, by 1865, about 10 percent of all slaves had learned how to read. Five percent had learned how to write.

Suzie King Taylor

Susie King Taylor was born into slavery in Georgia in 1848. She was the oldest of nine children. Although Georgia had strict laws against teaching slaves to read and write, she was educated at two secret schools taught by black women.

When the Civil War began, slaves began leaving their homes for areas where the Union Army was located, hoping to gain their freedom. In April 1862, 14-year-old Susie fled with other African Americans to St. Simons Island, off the coast of Georgia, which was occupied by Union forces. She soon set up a school for the children, becoming the first African American to teach openly in a school for former slaves in Georgia.

Suzie married an African-American soldier named Edward King in 1863, and traveled with the Union Army for the next three years. She worked as a nurse and also taught black soldiers how to read and write. She wrote, "I taught a great many of the comrades in Company E to read and write, when they were off duty. Nearly all were anxious to learn. . . . I was very happy to know my efforts were successful in camp, and also felt grateful for the appreciation of my services." Susie received no pay for her work.

After the war, Suzie ran another school for children in Georgia for a few years. When her husband died, she moved north to Boston, where she married a man named Russell Taylor. In 1902, she wrote a book about her experiences, titled *Reminiscences of My Life in Camp with the 33d United States Colored Troops Late 1st S. C. Volunteers*. Suzie King Taylor died in 1912.

It was time for even more to get an education.

Freed slaves were now able to set up more schools. Many of the schools they started were held in churches. Others were held in small, new school-houses. African Americans of all ages went to school. If parents could not attend, their children came home and taught them after school.

It is hard for a society to change, though. People hold on to old opinions. Slave owners who had lost their slaves after the Civil War were not happy. Many believed African Americans were not as smart as white people. They did not want blacks to go to school. They did not want African Americans to have any power. In the 1870s Southern states created "Black Codes." Black Codes were laws that limited the rights of freed slaves. They kept them from voting. They kept them from holding office or joining the military. They made it so poor

This detail from an 1865 illustration by the famous cartoonist Thomas Nast shows an idealized picture of an African-American mother sending her children off to a public school. After the abolition of slavery, blacks in the South did have greater opportunities to gain an education. Their right to attend school, work, and hold positions in government were protected by U.S. government soldiers. However, after the federal troops were withdrawn from the southern states in 1877, African Americans living there saw their rights gradually curtailed by the "Black Codes."

vagrants would be arrested. In addition, groups like the Ku Klux Klan tried to scare African Americans away from schools and voting places.

Still, former slaves worked hard to make new lives for themselves. The literacy rate among blacks in the South rose from 5 percent to 30 percent by the year 1880.

EARLY AFRICAN AMERICAN COLLEGES

In the 19th century, white Americans had many more chances to attend college than black Americans. White Americans had more money. More of them had a formal education that made it easier to be accepted into college. Most schools were segregated. This meant many colleges would not allow blacks to attend. African Americans would need their own colleges.

The First Congregational Society of Washington was a religious group. They met in November of 1866. They wanted to build a seminary to train African Americans to become ministers. Then they decided the school should teach more than ministers. It should become a university where students could study many different subjects.

The new university was named Howard University. This was in honor of General Oliver O. Howard. Howard had been a Civil War hero. He had also served as commissioner of the Freedman's Bureau. The Bureau gave the university money during its early years. The Bureau closed in 1872. However, in 1879, Congress decided to help fund the school. This way, it could continue to offer a good education to young African Americans.

═ Did You Know? ═

Mary Jane Patterson was the first African-American woman to receive a bachelor's degree from a college. She graduated from Oberlin College in 1862. She went on to teach school. Later she became principal of Dunbar High School in Washington, DC.

Today, Howard University teaches 10,500 students. More black students earn doctorate degrees on the Howard campus than at any other university in the world.

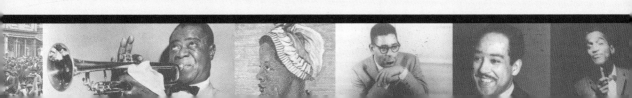

Modern view of Founders Library on the Howard University campus. The building, which opened in 1939, was designed by an African-American architect, Albert I. Cassell (1895-1969). Founders Library has been designated a National Historic Landmark.

In 1864, Union General William T. Sherman led his soldiers across Georgia. When they reached the city of Atlanta, they burned much of it. The city was left in ruins. Whites and blacks alike struggled to find places to live and food to eat. It was especially hard on the former slaves. They had little or no money.

In the fall of 1865, Frederick Ayers came to Atlanta. Ayers was a member of the American Missionary Association (AMA). Ayers was upset when he saw the great educational need of the former slaves. He and his wife started a school for them in an empty railroad boxcar. The Ayers and the students had few supplies. Yet they had a great determination to succeed. Over time this school grew to become Atlanta University.

Fisk University was founded Nashville in the fall of 1865. It was funded by the American Missionary Association. This school was first

— Did You Know? —

The American Missionary Association (AMA) was an organization that believed blacks and whites were equal. The AMA helped fund many schools for blacks after the Civil War.

opened to students ages seven to seventy. This gave former slaves, both children and adults, a chance to learn. Fisk was not only for blacks, however. With the AMA belief that all races were equal, whites and blacks attended together, The founders wanted the school to be measured by "the highest standards, not of Negro education, but of American education at its best."

Meharry Medical College was founded in 1876 in Nashville. It was the first medical school built in the South for African Americans. The college was named after the five Meharry brothers, Irish-born Americans who donated a great deal of money to the school. In 1877, the first student graduated from Meharry. The next year, three students received their degrees. The college grew. It continues to educate many medical students today.

Fisk University's landmark Jubilee Hall was built on the school's Nashville campus in 1876. Funds to build the hall were raised by the Fisk Jubilee Singers during a European singing tour in 1873.

SERVING THE PUBLIC

Black Codes made it illegal for African Americans in the South to do many things white people could do. Black Codes did not last long. Many were repealed, or were ended, in just a few years. However, this did not mean blacks were treated fairly. Many white slave owners were still angry that their slaves had been set free. They did not trust blacks. They did not want them to have equal rights.

This illustration from an 1866 issue of the popular magazine *Frank Leslie's Illustrated Newspaper* shows African-American women learning to sew in the Freedmen's Union Industrial School in Richmond, Virginia. The Freedmen's Bureau ran schools where reading, writing, and other basic school subjects were taught to both adults and children. These Freedmen's schools also taught vocational skills, like sewing. The ability to sew could enable black women to earn money as seamstresses, increasing their prospects of paid employment.

Matthew Gaines was an African American who was elected to the Texas State senate in 1869. Texas was a relatively new state. It had joined the Union in 1845. At the time of the Civil War, some parts of Texas had slaves, while other areas did not. After the Civil War, all the slaves in Texas and throughout the country were freed. African Americans celebrate this "freedom day," called Juneteenth, on June 19 each year.

More Land, More Opportunities

To build schools and colleges, there needs to be land. There needs to be money. Former slaves started some schools following the Civil War. Church congregations built schools. Cities and states opened other schools. Still, there were not enough schools for everyone.

Congress passed the Morrill Act in 1862. This act, named for Representative Justin Smith Morrill of Vermont (pictured at right) gave each state 30,000 acres of public land. The states were to sell the land. Then they were to use the money to build colleges.

Southern states did not use the money fairly. Most of it went to build colleges for white students. Little money went to colleges for black students. In 1890, a second Morrill Act was passed. Southern states had two choices. They could let black students attend the white colleges or they could build an equal number of colleges for black students. Sixteen new black colleges and universities were built because of the second Morrill Act. These include Alabama Agricultural and Mechanical University, Langston University in Oklahoma, South Carolina State University, and Southern University and A&M College in Louisiana.

= Did You Know? =

Edward A. Bouchet (1852–1918) attended Yale. In 1876 he became the first African American to earn a Ph.D from an American university. Because he was black, he could not get a job teaching in a mostly white college. He moved to Philadelphia to teach at the Institute for Colored Youth (now Cheyney University).

Unlike other Texas legislators, Gaines had been born into slavery. He spoke out with a strong voice on many issues that affected all people. One issue Senator Gaines felt was important was education. He helped pass a bill saying that schools and churches in Texas did not need to pay taxes. He supported the "Free School Bill," which he hoped would set up a public school system for black and white students. It required the state government to provide money for education.

However, part of the bill called for the integration of students. That part was taken out. Gaines was very disappointed. The "Free School Bill" helped pay for a new college to be built in Texas. It was called Agricultural and Mechanical College of Texas. (Today, the school is known as Texas A&M University). This was the first state-supported college in Texas.

Blacks did what they could to make a life for themselves after the Civil War. Many in the South worked as sharecroppers on the same land they had worked as slaves. Their country still did not see them as equals. Still, they did not give up. They contributed their hard work, talent, and knowledge to help the growing nation.

3

FIGHTING SEGREGATION AND DISCRIMINATION

After the Civil War, "Black Codes" were passed. These unfair laws denied freed slaves the rights that other citizens had. The codes only lasted several years. However, in the late 1870s, new laws were passed that were as bad as the Black Codes. Some were worse. They were meant to keep African Americans "in their place." They were meant to keep the races segregated, or separate from each other. These were called Jim Crow laws.

Some states passed laws that made it illegal for black and white children to go to school together. Other laws said that blacks had to ride in separate cars on trains, sit in different areas of restaurants, and even use different bathrooms and drinking fountains.

In 1896, the U.S. Supreme Court ruled that such state laws were acceptable. In a case known as *Plessy v. Ferguson*, the Court decided that states had the right to maintain "separate but equal" public facilities. That decision meant racial segregation was legal. In the years to come, the Plessy case would be used to argue against any future segregation cases brought before the courts.

Despite the Court's ruling, the separate facilities for blacks were never equal to those for whites. Because white communities had more

The U.S. Supreme Court's 1896 *Plessy v. Ferguson* decision made it legal to discriminate against African Americans by separating them from whites. (Top) A black man climbs the steps to the "colored" entrance at the rear of a movie theater in Mississippi. The lower door is labeled "white men only." (Left) An African-American man takes a drink from a "colored" water fountain. (Bottom right) A black man waits for a bus in an area separate from white passengers, Durham, North Carolina. Once on the bus, African Americans typically had to ride in the rear while whites could ride in the front. (Bottom left) Segregation was not limited to southern states, as this sign in the window of an Ohio restaurant indicates.

money, the schools for their children were better equipped. They had nicer buildings and could afford to hire more teachers. Schools for black children had little funding. Parents of these students donated money and time when they could. However, they had very little of either.

SPELMAN COLLEGE IS FOUNDED

In 1879, two women teachers from Massachusetts went south to Atlanta, Georgia. These women were Sophia B. Packard and Harriet E. Giles. They were members of the Woman's American Baptist Home Mission Society. It was their goal to find out how well African Americans were doing in the South.

A Closer Look at Jim Crow Laws

The name "Jim Crow" came from a character commonly featured in musical shows during the 1800s. "Jim Crow" was a stereotype of a black man. He sang and danced. He was not very smart. He was cheerful but lazy. A white man usually played "Jim Crow" wearing makeup, called blackface. White audiences thought this character was funny. Most black people probably did not.

Typical "Jim Crow" laws included the following:

1. Bus and train stations had to provide separate waiting rooms for blacks and whites.
2. Black persons could not be treated in the same hospital wards as whites.
3. Blacks and whites could not eat in the same room in a restaurant.
4. Blacks and whites could not be buried in the same area in a cemetery.

Packard and Giles were shocked by what they discovered. Most blacks were struggling to survive in the racist city. African Americans had few if any chances to get an education in Atlanta. This was especially true for women.

Packard and Giles returned to Boston. They were given $100 to start a school. Back in Atlanta, they found a room in the basement of Friendship Baptist Church. There, they offered lessons in writing and reading the Bible. The first class had eleven students. Ten were women. One was a young girl. Most of them were former slaves.

Over time, the two women raised more money. They bought a nine-acre piece of land. There were five frame buildings on the land. The land and buildings had been used during the Civil War to house and train soldiers. The school was named the Atlanta Baptist Female Seminary.

Over time, more money was raised. More students attended. In 1884, the school was named Spelman College. The Spelmans had been active in the anti-slavery movement. Spelman College continues to provide an excellent education to more than 2,100 students a year.

TUSKEGEE INSTITUTE

The same year that Spelman College was founded, Booker T. Washington founded Tuskegee Institute. This college was in Tuskegee, Alabama. It took a leading role in the education of African Americans.

Booker T. Washington was born into slavery in Virginia in 1856. Looking back, he showed his sense of humor when he said about his beginnings,

> I was born a slave on a plantation in Franklin County, Virginia. I am not quite sure of the exact place or exact date of my birth, but at any rate I suspect I must have been born somewhere and at some time.

Washington was seven years old when the Emancipation Proclamation freed the slaves. His family moved to West Virginia. They worked in the coal mines and salt furnaces. Washington returned to Virginia for an education. He attended Hampton Institute, a high school. It later grew to

Male and female students study in the library at Tuskegee Institute, circa 1902.

become Hampton University. When Washington graduated, he became a teacher.

Washington was an excellent teacher and speaker. He was invited to go to Alabama and start a new school for African Americans. Not only did Washington plan the school, he and his students built it themselves. Washington had three goals for students who attended Tuskegee.

1. To go back home after they graduated and share what they learned with others
2. To learn skills that would help them earn money and make a living
3. To become people of clean and good character

Booker T. Washington once said, "If you can't read, it's going to be hard to realize dreams." The famous educator spent his life working to create greater opportunities for African Americans.

Washington knew most of his students had had hard lives. He understood how they felt. He said,

> I suppose that every boy and every girl born in poverty have felt at some time in their lives the weight of the world against them. What the people in the communities did not expect them to do it was hard for them to convince themselves that they could do.

Washington wanted his students to believe that they were intelligent and could be successful. He believed that the most important things African Americans could learn were practical skills. Students at Tuskegee were taught trades. These included carpentry, farming, and brick making. Students raised their own food. They built new buildings when they were needed. They did almost everything themselves without help from others. This taught them to be self-confident and self-sufficient.

African Americans struggled in a world that did not treat them fairly. Booker T. Washington did not like that. He wanted whites to accept blacks as equal. However, he did not want them to be forced to do it. He believed that African Americans should make friends with whites. He thought they should work hard and make money. Whites would learn to respect them. Then they would earn the rights they did not have.

In 1895, Booker T. Washington gave a talk at the Cotton States Exposition in Atlanta. He shared his view that African Americans would gain the full rights of American citizenship through hard work. Washington believed that young African Americans should focus on getting an education that would prepare them for the kinds of agricultural or industrial jobs to be found in the South. Mastering work-related skills, he said, would enable African Americans to earn a good living. Through economic prosperity, blacks would show whites that they could be good citizens and reliable neighbors. He encouraged both black and white Southerners to "cast down your bucket where you are," meaning that if they could make the best of their current situation, things would get better in the future. Washington's speech was called the "Atlanta Compromise."

W.E.B. DuBOIS DISAGREES

Not everyone agreed with the ideas Washington expressed in his Atlanta speech. One of the most outspoken critics was W.E.B. DuBois. He had been born in Massachusetts in 1868, and was never a slave. Yet he came to know what it was like to be treated unfairly. When he was a young man he attended Fisk University in Nashville. There, he realized how bad African Americans were treated by the law and by white Southern society. After college, DuBois taught at Atlanta University for two years.

Unlike Booker T. Washington, DuBois thought African Americans should learn more than trade skills. He thought they should also study literature and art. They should learn other languages. They should take

After attending Fisk University, W.E.B. DuBois (1868–1963) was accepted at Harvard University. In 1895 he became the first African American to earn a Ph.D from Harvard.

the same subjects white students did. DuBois did not think blacks needed to prove themselves before they could gain the full rights of Americans. He thought they should demand them.

In 1905, DuBois and 29 others met in Buffalo, New York. They formed an organization called the Niagara Movement. The Niagara Movement created a "Declaration of Principals"—a list of things the members wanted. Some of these included the right to vote and the right to have a good, free education. They also wanted to be treated equally in public places. They wanted an end to "Jim Crow" laws.

DuBois spoke to the second meeting of the Niagara Movement. He said, in part,

> We want our children educated. The school system in the country districts of the South is a disgrace. . . . And when we call for education we mean real education. . . . We want our children trained as intelligent human beings should be. . . . We will never give up, though the trump of doom find us still fighting. And we shall win.

In 1909, members of the Niagara Movement and other groups interested in helping African Americans created the National Association for the Advancement of Colored People (NAACP). This new organization focused on fighting racial discrimination and worked for political and economic equality for blacks.

4

"WE MUST NOT FALTER"
FOLLOWING THE LEAD
OF GREAT THINKERS

On August 14, 1908, there was a riot in Springfield, Illinois. Whites had been told that a black man had attacked a white woman. The story was not true. Yet many white people believed it. They were angry. They turned their anger against the African Americans in the city. Homes and businesses were destroyed. Seven black people were killed. When it was over, only one white man what put on trial for theft. He was in jail 30 days. Then he was set free.

This violent event showed that there was still a lot of distrust between the races, even in the Northern states. In the court system there was not equal justice for blacks.

Mary White Ovington lived in a black neighborhood in New York City. She was a white woman. She was there to learn about the living conditions of African Americans. Ovington read about the Springfield riot and trial in the paper. It upset her. In 1909 she got together in New York with others who were also upset. They talked about what could be done to make things better for African Americans. She later wrote:

> It was then that the National Association for the Advancement of Colored People was born. It was born in a little room of a New York apartment.

Others were invited to help with the National Association for the Advancement of Colored People (NAACP). Some had been part of the Niagara Movement, such as W.E.B. DuBois. DuBois was a strong speaker and writer. His speeches and his writings demanded change. Many white Americans did not like what the NAACP stood for. However, the organization became a leader in gaining civil rights for minorities.

FROM MINER TO EDUCATOR

Carter G. Woodson was born in Virginia in 1875. He did not get to go to school as a young person. He had to work in the coal mines. He taught himself to read a little. He moved to West Virginia and started school when he was 20 years old. A very smart young man, he finished high school in just two years.

After high school Woodson went to Berea College and the University of

Chicago. Then he attended Harvard University. He became the second African American to earn a Ph. D in history, following Dubois.

Woodson had noticed that something was missing in American schools. Black and white students both studied history. They studied the history of the Greeks. They studied the history of the Romans. They learned the history of Europeans and Americans. Yet no classes taught the history of Africans or African Americans. Woodson would help change that.

In 1915, Woodson founded the Association for the Studies of Afro-American life. He wanted to learn all he could about the history of his people. He began the *Journal of Negro History*.

Carter G. Woodson (1875–1950) is sometimes called the "father of Black History."

This journal gathered and shared little-known facts about black history.

Woodson spent his life publishing black history. In 1926 he founded Negro History Week. This later became what is now Black History Month.

Teaching African American history in American schools was a main goal for Woodson. He believed it was wrong to ignore an important part of the past. In 1927 he wrote, "The fact is that the so-called history teaching in our schools and colleges is downright propaganda, an effort to praise one race and to decry the other." Throughout his life, Woodson helped bring African-American history into American classrooms.

FROM COTTON PICKER TO EDUCATIONAL LEADER

Mary McLeod Bethune's mother was a slave. She was freed with the passing of the Thirteenth Amendment. Mary was born in 1875 and grew up on her mother's rice and cotton farm. Mary said, "When I was only nine, I could pick 250 pounds of cotton a day."

As a child, when she wasn't working, Bethune walked several miles to school. It was the only school that would admit her. The school was run by missionaries. Mary was a good student. She learned quickly. She knew that many other children like her were not able to go to school. She realized it was especially hard for girls.

In 1904, Mary had just $1.50. She took the money and moved to Daytona, Florida. There, she raised a little more money and rented a four-room cottage. She started a school for girls. It was called the Daytona Educational and Industrial School for Negro Girls. Five students attended the first year.

The cottage was in bad shape. The school had few supplies. Bethune bought what she could afford. The rest she begged for. Sometimes the students used burned splinters as pencils.

The school grew. Bethune was a good teacher. More parents sent their children. In less than two years, there were 250 students. An addition was built onto the cottage. Over time, more money was raised. Bethune bought land and the school moved. It later merged with another school, the

Mary McLeod Bethune (1875–1955) is pictured in her office at Daytona Beach, Florida. Bethune-Cookman College, circa 1943.

Cookman Institute, and was renamed Bethune-Cookman College. (It became Bethune-Cookman University in 2007.)

Bethune worked throughout her life to help African Americans and women. One day she met leader and educator W.E.B. DuBois. She heard him tell how he was not able to check his own books out of a Southern library. This inspired her to start the first library in Florida that was open to all citizens regardless of race.

From 1936 to 1944, Bethune was director of the Division of Negro Affairs of the National Youth Administration. She was the first black woman to be named as the head of a federal agency. Later she served with the United Nations. Her comment about African American women applied to herself as well as others:

> As the years have gone on the Negro woman has touched the most vital fields in the civilization of today. Wherever she had contributed she has left the mark of a strong character. The educational institutions she has established and directed have met the needs of her young people. . . . She has made and is making history.

STUDENT, SCHOLAR, AND INSPIRATION

Alain LeRoy Locke was born in Philadelphia in 1886. His parents were both teachers. After high school, Locke went to Harvard University. He was named the first African American Rhodes Scholar in 1907. A Rhodes scholar is someone who receives a Rhodes Scholarship to attend Oxford University in England. It is only given to the very best university students.

After studying in England, Locke went to Germany. There he attended the University of Berlin. He learned a great deal while studying abroad, and was able to see how people of different races were treated in other countries.

In 1912, Locke returned to the United States. He took a job at Harvard in the Philosophy Department. He became department head in 1921 and taught there for 41 years. While there, Locke wrote and edited many books. He was very interested in social science, the study of how people get along and relate to each other. He was also very interested in literature, music, and art. He believed that when America began to appreciate the art, literature, and music of its black citizens, blacks would be accepted as equals.

Locke shared the music, art, and literature of African Americans through his books. This helped bring about the "Harlem Renaissance."

The New Negro

Alain Locke's book *The New Negro* was published in 1926. In it, Locke wrote that attitudes about African Americans had changed over time. He wrote that for many years, blacks had been "something to be argued about, condemned or defended, to be 'kept down' or 'in his place' or 'helped up,' to be worried with or worried over." Yet over the years, Locke wrote, blacks had gained a new self-understanding. A new pride had arisen. By the 1920s, many African Americans no longer saw themselves as children of slaves. They had grown strong from what they had gone through in the past. Now, they were speaking and singing out to share their experiences with the world. Locke's book was an inspiration to many black Americans.

THE HARLEM RENAISSANCE

New York City was a huge, busy city in the early 1900s. People from many places around the world lived there. Some of these people had been in the city for generations. Others had moved to New York from Europe and Asia. Usually, people lived in neighborhoods where others from their home countries lived. They felt more comfortable this way.

Harlem was a New York district. At one time, many wealthy white families had lived there, but by the early 1900s most of them had left. African Americans began moving into Harlem. Many came from the South looking for a better way of life. In Harlem, African Americans found that new life. They became professionals and artists. They became businessmen and women. They were also free to share their art, music, literature, and drama.

Jazz and blues music became very popular in Harlem. The writings of black authors and poets were published and shared. There were dances and plays. There were readings for people to attend. It was a cultural explosion. Some of the music, art, and literature became popular with whites, too. They came to have a better appreciation of black history, culture, and pride. This cultural explosion, known as the Harlem Renaissance, lasted from about 1919 until the middle of the 1930s.

> **= Did You Know? =**
>
> In 1944, Frederick Douglass Patterson, then president of Tuskegee Institute, started the United Negro College Fund. This fund provides money to black colleges. It also gives scholarships to worthy black students.

EDUCATOR, POET, AND SONGWRITER

James Weldon Johnson was born in 1871. His family had plenty of money. His father was a headwaiter in Jacksonville, Florida. His mother was Florida's first female African-American public school teacher. James Johnson was a good student. He especially enjoyed reading and music.

As a young man, Johnson attended Atlanta University. During the summers he took a job as a teacher in Hampton, Georgia. The students he taught were very poor. He had never spent much time with poor black people before. He was saddened by what he saw. He wanted to make a difference. When he graduated from the university, he went back to Florida.

In Florida he became principal of the school where his mother had taught. He worked hard. He wanted to make sure his students got a good education. He also started a newspaper, the *Daily American*. This newspaper was founded to help black adults who were poor learn to read. It also helped them find out about what was going on in the world. In his spare time, Johnson stud-

Educator, writer, and activist James Weldon Johnson (1871–1938) was one of the first African-American professors at New York University.

ied law. He was the first African American to become a lawyer in the state of Florida.

Johnson never lost his interest in music. He and his brother, John, began writing music together. In 1902, Johnson quit his job as principal. He and John moved to New York City. They became successful composers.

Popular music of the time showed African Americans in much the same negative way that the minstrel show "Jim Crow" character had years earlier. Johnson did not like this. He decided to focus on writing poetry and books. His first collection of poems was *Fifty Years and Other Poems*. It was published in 1917. Johnson went on to write many important books about African-American life. One was a history of the Harlem Renaissance. It was called *Black Manhattan*.

Activist Daisy Bates (1914–1999), who coordinated the integration of Little Rock's Central High School in 1957–58, is pictured with the first school's first nine African-American students, known as the "Little Rock Nine": (front, left to right) Thelma Mothershed, Minnijean Brown, Elizabeth Eckford, Gloria Ray, (back) Jefferson Thomas, Melba Pattillo, Terrence Roberts, Carlotta Walls, Bates, and Ernest Green. (Bottom) Angry whites protest against the integration of Central High School outside the Arkansas state capitol.

5

"INHERENTLY UNEQUAL"
STRIKING DOWN SEGREGATION

O n December 7, 1941, Japanese planes attacked the American Naval Base in Pearl Harbor, Hawaii. This caused the United States to enter World War II. The war had begun in 1939. There was fighting in both Europe and Asia. White and black American soldiers went overseas. Some fought the Germans in Europe. Others fought the Japanese in the Pacific region. Yet American troops were kept apart from each other. Whites and blacks did not serve side by side. When the war was over, American soldiers returned home. More than one million of the veterans were African Americans.

The United States government wanted to help the veterans. They had given so much of themselves for their country. On June 22, 1944, Congress passed the G.I. Bill. This bill made money available to the veterans. They could use the money to find housing. They could use it to go to college or get job training.

Both white and black veterans were able to apply for the money. However, fewer blacks were able to make use of the money. It was especially hard for those living in the South. African-American veterans in the southern states had fewer colleges from which to choose. Most colleges were still segregated. Colleges that did admit blacks did not have enough

room for all who wanted to attend. Also, there were fewer government counselors in the South to help the vets apply for money.

SEPARATE BUT EQUAL CHALLENGED

Schools in the 1950s were much like they were in the past. Public schools for white students received much more money than schools for black students. Schools for African Americans often got old textbooks when white students were through with them. Furniture was rarely new. Needed repairs were not made quickly or at all.

A black child might live close to a school for white children. He still could not go there. He would have to travel to the nearest school for black children. It might be miles away. The majority of white citizens thought this was fine. It seemed as if they didn't care or didn't notice the unfairness. It seemed as if they felt their children were worth more than African American children.

= Did You Know? =

In 1955, the Board of Education in Georgia made a serious threat. They said they would take away the teaching license of any teacher who was caught teaching a class with both white and black students.

All this was challenged in the fall of 1950. Oliver Brown lived in Topeka, Kansas. His daughter, Linda, was seven years old. Linda was a student at Monroe. It was a school for African American children. Oliver Brown and several other black families tried to enroll their children in a white school. They were told no.

BROWN V. BOARD OF EDUCATION

Oliver Brown and the other families sued the Topeka board of education. He had help from the NAACP. The organization provided him with good lawyers. They argued that "separate but equal" was hardly ever equal. They said school segregation was wrong. They lost the case.

The NAACP appealed the decision, and it was eventually referred to the U.S. Supreme Court. The NAACP lawyers said that black students

In 1954 there were no African Americans serving as justices on the U.S. Supreme Court. The first black Supreme Court justice was not appointed until 1967, when Thurgood Marshall—who had argued the Brown case in 1954—was appointed to the high court.

were not being treated equally under the law. All citizens had the right to equal protection, they argued. On May 17, 1954, the Supreme Court issued its ruling in the case of *Brown v. Board of Education of Topeka, Kansas*. It said school segregation was not legal.

Earl Warren, the court's chief justice, explained the ruling. He wrote, "We conclude that in the field of public education the doctrine of 'separate but equal' has no place. Separate educational facilities are inherently unequal."

A victory had been won. All schools in the United States would need to let both white and black students attend.

SOUTHERN RESISTANCE

Central High School was an all white school in Little Rock, Arkansas. In 1954 the Supreme Court ordered states to integrate their public schools. Many areas in the South refused. Little Rock was one city that did not want to let black students and white students attend the same schools.

On September 3, 1957, nine African-American students arrived at Little Rock's Central High School for the first day of school. The governor of Arkansas sent the National Guard to stop the students. President Dwight D. Eisenhower tried to get the governor to allow the students to enroll. The governor refused.

President Eisenhower sent 1,000 soldiers to Central High School on September 25. They kept back an angry crowd of white people. The nine black students were able to enter the school. They became known as the Little Rock Nine.

Melba Pattillo Beals was one of the Little Rock Nine. She was asked what it was like her first year at Central High. She said:

> In the beginning, a few of the white students reached out to us. They smiled, they wanted to talk to us. They actually tried to befriend us. But as September turned into October, these few souls were crushed in the machinery set up by segregationists to separate us, to torture us until we left the school. Physically and mentally tortured us. So within a short amount of time these white students had to cut off from us to save themselves. Otherwise they, too, would be ostracized by the segregationists. They had to turn away from us. This was the case throughout the year.

Other states refused to integrate. In 1956, Autherine Lucy tried to enroll in the University of Alabama. Mobs gathered on campus. They threw eggs at her. They shouted threats. Lucy was escorted off campus in a police car so she would not get hurt.

Lucy had been told by the court that she could go to the university. The NAACP had helped her win her case. One of her lawyers was Thurgood Marshall, who later became a Supreme Court Justice. However, the danger made Lucy decide not to go to the university.

Virginia, South Carolina, Mississippi, and other states also resisted integration for many years. South Carolina did not fully integrate all of its public schools until 1970.

MAKING INTEGRATION WORK

Integrating schools was difficult. For hundreds of years, most white and black Americans had lived separate lives. They did not eat together. They did not attend the same churches. They did not marry each other. They did not go to the same schools.

When the the Supreme Court ruled in 1954 that segregating schools

was wrong, many white people resisted. Black students knew they would face trouble in white schools. However, dedicated people did what they could to make integration happen as smoothly as possible.

One such person was Mozell Hill. He was born in Alabama in 1911. Hill taught at both Langston University and Atlanta University. Hill was very interested in sociology. Sociology is the study of human society and its problems. Hill studied African American communities and education. He learned a lot about the lives of black people in the United States. His book *Culture of a Contemporary Negro Community* was published in 1946.

When it was time for American schools to integrate, Hill wanted to do his part. He helped write a book called *The Negro and the Schools*. This book has also been called the "Ashmore Report." This report took a close look at segregation in the South. It helped others see the effects of keep-

School Closure in Virginia

In 1959, Prince Edward County in Virginia decided to close its public schools rather than integrate them. White students were still able to get an education in private schools. The state of Virginia even provided grant money to fund these private schools. However, there was no state money for private schools for black students.

Some African-American parents sent their children to live with relatives in other parts of Virginia, or even other states, where schools for blacks were still open. Some children who stayed in Prince Edward County attended schools that black teachers opened in church basements. However, other African-American children received no formal education at all during the next five years.

Prince Edward County was forced to reopen its public schools in 1964, after the U.S. Supreme Court ruled that the state of Virginia could not give grant money to private schools.

In 1962 James Meredith (center) became the first African American to enroll at the University of Mississippi. For his protection, he had to be escorted across campus by U.S. marshals.

ing the races apart. The information in the book was useful in planning ways to integrate schools and other public places.

Teachers and other adults weren't the only ones who worked to end segregation. Students did, too. On February 1, 1960, black college students in North Carolina went to Greensboro, North Carolina. They sat down at a lunch counter. This lunch counter was for whites only. They were ordered to leave. They didn't. They sat there. Even when others poured drinks on them and screamed at them they stayed put. This became known as a "sit in."

Other African American college students heard about this. They staged their own "sit ins" in Southern towns. People around the nation heard and read about the "sit ins." Some people agreed with the students. Some did not.

In April 1960, 200 students got together at Shaw University in Raleigh, NC. They formed the Student Nonviolent Coordinating Committee (SNCC). These students spoke and acted out against segregation. They spoke and acted out against injustice. They did not believe in the use of violence. In this way, they were much like the famous civil rights leader, Martin Luther King, Jr. These young people inspired others to stand up for their rights as citizens.

6

EDUCATION TODAY
PROGRESS AND PROBLEMS

In 1954 the Supreme Court ruled that having different schools for different races was wrong. Schools across the United States had to open their doors to both white and black students.

Integrating schools offered many good things. Black students could now go to a closer school even if it had once been for whites only. Black students now had better books. They had use of better materials. They now could attend schools that were in good condition. According to the law, African American students were as important as white students. By the early 1970s most all public schools were open to all students.

Yet there were problems. Black students did not always feel welcome. Some were picked on by white students. Others felt they had lost something important when they left their old school. Former FBI agent Eugene Perry, Jr. was a young student in Waynesboro, Virginia in the 1950s and 1960s. He first attended Rosenwald School. Rosenwald was a school for black students. Waynesboro schools integrated in the mid-1960s. Perry had to leave Rosenwald and go to the once all-white Kate Collins School. He said,

> It was like going to another world. My parents, aunts, and uncles had all attended Rosenwald. I'd dreamed of being Valedictorian of my graduating class like my mother had been . . . But my dreams went up in smoke."

Black and white students ride a school bus from the suburbs to an inner-city school in Charlotte, North Carolina, February 1973. Two years earlier, in the case *Swann v. Charlotte-Mecklenburg Board of Education*, the U.S. Supreme Court had ruled that black students could be bused to white schools, and vice-versa, to change the racial makeup of the schools and fulfill the constitutional requirement that public schools be desegregated. During the 1970s and 1980s, desegregation busing remained a highly controversial topic.

Some African American teachers lost their jobs. Others were given jobs in the integrated schools. These teachers brought their knowledge and talents with them. They were ready to teach all students no matter what race they were. Some of these teachers were welcomed. Others were not.

One African American teacher went to her new job at an integrated school. She found that all the black students were put into only one of her classes. In this way, the school still tried to keep black and white students apart. Another black teacher in Texas was assigned to teach in an integrated school. The principal told her, "You're the best teacher I have in the system, black or white. I did not have to tell you that and if you tell anyone I said that, I'm gonna tell 'em you lied. Do you get my meaning?"

Through it all, many of the African-American teachers did their best. They gave of themselves and tried to teach all their students well.

THE NATIONAL ALLIANCE OF BLACK SCHOOL EDUCATORS

In 1968, Dr. Charles D. Moody was named the first African-American school superintendent of schools in Harvey, Illinois. A veteran of the U.S. Army who had been born in Louisiana and educated as a science teacher at Chicago Teachers College, Dr. Moody said he wanted to help make schools better for black teachers and students.

In 1970, Moody invited other African-American school superintendents from around the country to meet and discuss problems they faced as black educators in a mainly white nation. They talked about things they could do to improve their schools. Dr. Moody said, "When one is in a struggle or battle, he looks around to see if he is alone."

Fifteen of the other superintendents agreed it would be good to form an organization to help them. The group they formed is now known as the National Alliance of Black School Superintendents (NABSE.) The NABSE is "dedicated to improving both the educational experiences and accomplishments of African American youths" by improving instruction and increasing motivation. Today, the NABSE has more than 10,000 educator members. It

Did You Know?

Educators are finding fast and even fun ways to get in touch with each other. Many now use the Internet to share ideas and information. For example, on Facebook there are groups for African American teachers in different states. There are groups for black teachers of music, math, and other subjects.

offers conferences, tutors, training, scholarships, student trips, and more.

MARVA COLLINS'S MISSION

Marva Collins was born in Monroeville, Alabama in 1936. When she was growing up, Jim Crow laws prevented African-Americans from using the public library or from using water fountains restricted for white people only. Her school had few books; the ones they did have were castoffs from the white schools. There were no indoor toilets in her school. Her grandfather was a successful businessman despite segregation and he encouraged her to do well in school and to be independent.

Collins graduated from Clark College in Atlanta. She taught school in Alabama for two years, then moved to Chicago.

The schools in Chicago troubled Collins, because of the poor quality of education children were receiving. They were treated as if they didn't matter. They were not learning because their teachers didn't believe they could succeed. Collins believed the students could learn and, indeed, they did in her classroom. She tried to make changes in her school. However, none of the educators wanted to listen to her ideas. In disgust, Collins decided to start her own school.

In 1975, Collins took her entire savings of $5,000 from her teacher retirement account. She used it to start a school in her home. She called it the Westside Preparatory School. At first she only had six students. Soon, more children enrolled in her school. They were black children from families with very little money. Some were called "problem" students at their other schools. They were not expected to learn much. At the end of the first year, these children scored high on standardized tests that were administered and graded independently. In fact, all of the children had gained five academic grades in just one year!

Marva Collins once said, "There is a brilliant child locked inside every student." Her Westside Preparatory School was widely praised for its success in teaching children from poor, inner-city Chicago families. Collins has written many books about educational techniques, and often speaks about her experiences.

Collins encouraged her students to share their opinions. They read books that other people thought were too difficult for children to read. They learned to compare their views with the views of others and they learned how to do this with logical reasoning. They learned to question everything they read. The students gained confidence in themselves. Collins knew they could do well. She expected them to, and they did.

The Westside Preparatory School was open from 1975 until 2008. Many of Collins' students went on to be teachers, doctors, engineers, and lawyers. Collins became well known for her successes. She has been featured twice on the television program *60 Minutes*. She has received presidential awards and many honorary degrees from colleges such as Dartmouth and Notre Dame. She shares her methods of teaching around the country and overseas so that teachers can use her program and methods in their own classrooms.

ELMA LEWIS'S DREAM

Elma Lewis loved the arts. She believed that music and dance were important. They helped people connect with their culture. Lewis wanted young African Americans to have a chance to study them. Yet in 1950, there

seemed to be little interest in having special arts schools for black students.

Lewis lived in Boston. There was no public money for a school of the arts. This did not stop her. Like some other dedicated African American teachers before her, she opened a school herself. First it was held in an apartment. Then it moved to a synagogue and school nearby. Lewis named it the Elma Lewis School of Fine Arts.

Lewis was a strict teacher. She expected a lot from her students. She taught them to dance. She taught them to sing. She taught them to perform on stage in musical theater. Most of her students had come from poor families. They worked hard and did well. Many went on to careers on Broadway or in other theaters.

The Elma Lewis School of Fine Arts continued to grow. It became well known around the nation. In 1968, Lewis founded the National Center of Afro-American Artists (NCAAA). This organization invited famous dancers, composers, musicians, and actors to Boston. The professionals and students met with each other. They learned from each other and learned with each other. Over the years, Lewis' center became known around the world. Lewis and her students brought African American culture to people who had never experienced it before. She said:

> My work is a widening of the spirit. Each person's own creativity frees him if he is permitted to use it. Our society doesn't encourage that. It certainly was not encouraged among blacks. I encouraged my students to go way inside and find that deep wellspring and follow it where it leads, no matter what anyone says.

GEOFFREY CANADA'S HOPES

Geoffrey Canada grew up in the South Bronx, New York. His family had very little. He often did not have enough food to eat. There was violence and crime in his neighborhood. Yet even as a young boy, he knew what he wanted to do when he grew up. He wanted to help the people who lived where he lived.

Canada did well in high school. He got a scholarship to Bowdoin College. Then he attended Harvard. He received a master's degree in edu-

cation. For a short while he taught troubled students in Boston. He went back to New York in 1990.

Canada was put in charge of an education center in Harlem. The center was in the middle of a troubled neighborhood. There was violence. There were drugs. Students dropped out of school. Canada knew he had a big challenge ahead.

To make a difference, there needed to be a change. Canada changed the name of the center to the Harlem Children's Zone (HCZ). Then he changed the way the center operated. He knew that to help at-risk students, he needed to help their families, too. He did just that.

During the day, students took classes. The classes were kept small so students would get more individual attention. At night, programs were offered to families and other members of the community. Private donations helped the Harlem Children's Zone grow. Students did well in the school. They still do. As of 2010, 90 percent of public school students who took part in programs at HCZ were able to get into college.

Of his students, Canada has said, "These kids are going to graduate . . . they are going to have a good life, their children are going to have a good life."

Canada's hopes are much the same as African-American educators who came before him. They wanted to give the best to their students. Those who teach now want the same thing.

CHAPTER NOTES

p. 12:   "Punishment for teaching slaves or . . ." from *Slave Codes of the State of Georgia, 1848*, reprinted at http://academic.udayton.edu/race/02rights/slavelaw.htm#11.

p. 12:   "While in the South I . . .", Lunsford Lane, *The Narrative of Lunsford Lane, Formerly of Raleigh, N.C.* (reprinted in electronic edition, 1999), p. 4. http://docsouth.unc.edu/neh/lanelunsford/lane.html

p. 13:   "O, how I longed to die . . ." Lily Ann Granderson, quoted in *A Woman's Life-Work* by Laura S. Haviland, 1881 (reprinted by AYER Company Publishers, Inc, 1984), p. 300

p. 14:   "Dark and thorny is the pathway . . ." Negro spiritual of the time of the Underground Railroad, reprinted at http://mconn.doe.state.la.us/lessonplans.php?task=LP_view&lesson_id=6746&dispPage=1

p. 15:   "so great a desire for knowledge . . .", Charlotte Forten, "Life on the Sea Islands," *The Atlantic Monthly* 13 (May and June 1864), pp. 587-96.

p. 15:   "The first day of school was . . ." Forten, "Life on the Sea Islands," pp. 666-76.

p. 17:   "I taught a great many . . ." Susie King Taylor, *Reminiscences of My Life in Camp with the 33d United States Colored Troops Late 1st S.C. Volunteers* (Boston: published by the author, 1902), p. 21.

p. 21:   "the highest standards, not of Negro education . . ." "Fisk's Storied Past," Fish University official website. http://www.fisk.edu/AboutFisk/HistoryOfFisk.aspx

p. 28:   "I was born a slave . . ." Booker T. Washington, quoted on the Booker T. Washington National Monument site, National Park Service http://www.nps.gov/bowa/historyculture/index.htm

p. 30:   "I suppose that every boy . . ." Booker T. Washington, in the *Booker T. Washington Papers, Volume I, Autobiographical Writings*, Louis R. Harlan, ed., (Urbana and Chicago, University of Illinois Press, 1972), p. 422.

p. 31:   "cast down your bucket where you are," Booker T. Washington, *Booker T. Washington Papers, Volume V, 1899-1900*, Louis R. Harlan, ed., (Urbana and Chicago, University of Illinois Press, 1972), p. 50.

p. 32:   "We want our children educated . . ." W.E.B. DuBois, "Address to the Nation," on the TeachingAmericanHistory.org website. http://teachingamericanhistory.org/library/index.asp?document=496

p. 33:   "We Must Not Falter, . . ." W.E.B DuBois, "Niagara Movement Speech" (1905), on the TeachingAmericanHistory.org website. http://teachingamericanhistory.org/library/index.asp?document=496

p. 33:   "It was then that . . ." Mary White Ovington, quoted on the NAACP website. http://www.naacphistory.org/#/home

p. 35:   "The fact that the so-called . . ." Carter G. Woodson, quoted from his letter on the Freeman Institute website. http://www.freemaninstitute.com/woodson.htm

p. 35:   "When I was only nine . . ." Mary McLeod Bethune, quoted in Russell, *Black Genius*, p 170.

p. 36:   "As the years have gone . . ." Mary McLeod Bethune, quoted in Dick Russell, *Black Genius* (New York: Carroll & Graf, 1998), p.169.

p. 37:   "something to be argued about . . ." Alain Locke, introduction to *The New Negro* (New York: Albert and Charles Boni, Inc., 1925) p. 3.

p. 43:   "We conclude that in . . ." Chief Justice Earl Warren, from the opinion of the Supreme Court of the United States, *Brown et. al. v. Board of Education of Topeka et. al*, May 17, 1954.

p. 44:   "In the beginning, a few of the . . ." Melba Pattillo Beals, from an interview posted on the Scholastic, Inc. website. http://www2.scholastic.com/browse/article.jsp?id=4799

p. 47:   "It was like going to . . ." Eugene Perry Jr., quoted in Elizabeth Spilman Massie and Cortney Skinner, *Images of America: Waynesboro* (Charleston, S.C., Arcadia Publishing, 2009), p. 67.

p. 49:   "You're the best teacher I have . . ." Ella Jane, quoted in Kathleen Weiler and Candace Mitchell, eds., *What Schools Can Do: Critical Pedagogy and Practice* (Albany: State University of New York Press, 1992), p.186.

p. 49:   "When one is in a struggle . . ." Dr. Charles D. Moody, quoted on the NABSE website. http://www.nabse.org/

p. 51:   "There is a brilliant child locked . . ." Marva Collins, quoted on America's Promise Alliance website, http://www.americaspromise.org/About-the-Alliance/Press-

Room/Speeches-and-Quotes/2009-Alma-March-5.aspx

p. 52:   "My work is a widening . . ." Elma Lewis, quoted in Russell, *Black Genius*, p. 177.

p. 49:   "dedicated to improving both . . ." National Alliance of Black School Educators website, http://www.nrccua.org/cms/mailing/services/nabse.

p. 53:   "These kids are going to graduate . . ." Geoffrey Canada, quoted in Jacob Osterhout, "*Waiting for Superman's* Geoffrey Canada, president of Harlem's Children Zone, talks education," *New York Daily News* (September 22, 2010).

CHRONOLOGY

1862: Charlotte Forten becomes the first African American to leave the North and teach former slaves in the South.

1865: The Thirteenth Amendment, declaring all slaves free, is ratified in December. The Freedman's Bureau is set up the assist former slaves with jobs, food, and education.

1869: Matthew Gaines is elected to the Texas State Senate and works to improve education for both blacks and whites.

1876: Meharry College, the first medical school for African Americans in the South, is founded.

1879: Sophia B. Packard and Harriet E. Giles found Spelman College and Booker T. Washington founds Tuskegee Institute.

1905: W.E.B. DuBois and others meet to form the Niagara movement and create a list of the rights African Americans deserve.

1909: The NAACP is founded to help create social equality for blacks, on February 12.

1919: The Harlem Renaissance, a time of great cultural and artistic expression of African Americans living in Harlem, begins; it lasts until the mid-1930s.

1926: Carter G. Woodson establishes Negro History Week, which later became Black History Month, in February.

1954: In May, the U.S. Supreme Court rules in *Brown v Board of Education* that school segregation is unconstitutional.

1970: Dr. Charles D. Moody founds the National Alliance of Black School Educators.

1975: Marva Collins opens the Westside Preparatory School for disadvantaged black children in Chicago

1990: Geoffrey Canada takes over an education center in Harlem and converts it to the Harlem Children's Zone, where children get schooling as well as medical and social services.

GLOSSARY

abolish—to get rid of completely.

bi-racial—concerning or having aspects of two different races.

cash crops—crops grown to sell.

civil rights—the rights of all citizens, right that are protected by law.

descendants—a person who is descended from another, such as a son, grandson, or great-grandson.

discrimination—the act of treating people or things in different ways because of prejudice.

forge—to make something false that can be passed off as real.

inferior—not as good as something else.

integration—the act of bringing different things or people together.

literacy—the ability to read and write.

majority—the larger part or number; more than half.

Ph.D—a doctorate degree, the highest college degree.

propaganda—the spreading of information in a way that makes people agree with the information.

racist—prejudiced against someone because of his or her race.

renaissance—a renewed interest or revival of music, art, literature, and learning.

segregated—kept apart based on race.

segregationists—people who want to keep the races separate from each other

seminary—a school that trains ministers or priests.

stereotype—a widely held view of someone or something based on general ideas that may or may not be true.

vagrants—people without homes or regular jobs who wander from place to place.

FURTHER READING

Beals, Melba Pattillo. *Warriors Don't Cry*. New York: Simon Pulse, 2007.

Bolden, Tonya. *W.E.B. DuBois Up Close*. New York: Viking Juvenile, 2008.

Cothram, John C. *A Search of American American Life, Achievement and Culture*. Carrollton, Texas: Stardate Publishing Company, 2006.

Cox, Clinton. *Black Stars: African American Teachers*. New York: John Wiley and Sons, 2000.

Forten, Charlotte. "Life on the Sea Islands," *The Atlantic Monthly*, May and June, 1864.

Hill, Laban Carrick. *Harlem Stomp!: A Cultural History of the Harlem Renaissance*. Boston: Little, Brown Books for Young Readers, 2009.

Painter, Nell Irvin. *Creating Black Americans*. New York: Oxford University Press, 2006.

Tate, Eleanora. *Celeste's Harlem Renaissance*. Boston: Little, Brown Books for Young Readers, 2009.

Wukovits, John. *Booker T. Washington and Education*. San Diego: Lucent Books, 2008.

INTERNET RESOURCES

http://www.naacp.org/content/main/

The official website of the National Association for the Advancement of Colored People (NAACP) shares the history of the organization as well as its current programs and services.

http://docsouth.unc.edu/fpn/washington/bio.html

The University of North Carolina's website regarding Booker T. Washington gives a brief history of this African American educator.

http://www.pbs.org/wnet/jimcrow/stories_people_dubois.html

This PBS website offers a biography of W.E.B. DuBois.

http://www.nps.gov/mamc/index.htm

The National Park Service website for Mary McLeod Bethune tells about her life and the historic site of her Council House.

http://www.marvacollins.com/biography.html

The Marva Collins Seminars website features a biography of the educator.

http://www.hcz.org/

Official website for the Harlem Children's Zone, featuring information on Geoffrey Canada and his work with the center.

INDEX

Numbers in **bold italics** refer to captions.

CONTRIBUTORS

ELIZABETH MASSIE is a former middle school teacher who now is a free-lance writer and creative writing instructor. Her works for young readers include the YOUNG FOUNDERS series (Tor), the DAUGHTERS OF LIBERTY trilogy (Pocket Books), *The Fight For Right* (Steck-Vaughn), *Back From the Edge* (Zaner-Bloser), and other books.

Senior Consulting Editor **DR. MARC LAMONT HILL** is one of the leading hip-hop generation intellectuals in the country. Dr. Hill has lectured widely and provides regular commentary for media outlets like NPR, the *Washington Post*, *Essence Magazine*, the *New York Times*, CNN, MSNBC, and *The O'Reilly Factor*. He is the host of the nationally syndicated television show *Our World With Black Enterprise*. Dr. Hill is a columnist and editor-at-large for the *Philadelphia Daily News*. His books include the award-winning *Beats, Rhymes, and Classroom Life: Hip-Hop Pedagogy and the Politics of Identity* (2009).

Since 2009 Dr. Hill has been on the faculty of Columbia University as Associate Professor of Education at Teachers College. He holds an affiliated faculty appointment in African American Studies at the Institute for Research in African American Studies at Columbia University.

Since his days as a youth in Philadelphia, Dr. Hill has been a social justice activist and organizer. He is a founding board member of My5th, a non-profit organization devoted to educating youth about their legal rights and responsibilities. He is also a board member and organizer of the Philadelphia Student Union. Dr. Hill also works closely with the ACLU Drug Reform Project, focusing on drug informant policy. In addition to his political work, Dr. Hill continues to work directly with African American and Latino youth.

In 2005, *Ebony* named Dr. Hill one of America's 100 most influential Black leaders. The magazine had previously named him one of America's top 30 Black leaders under 30 years old.